Ultimate Cars

CORVETTE

A.T. McKenna
ABDO Publishing Company

visit us at
www.abdopub.com

Published by Abdo Publishing Company, 4940 Viking Drive, Edina, Minnesota 55435.
Copyright © 2000 by Abdo Consulting Group, Inc. International copyrights reserved in all countries. No part of this book may be reproduced in any form without written permission from the publisher.

Printed in the United States.

Cover and Interior Photo credits: Corbis, AP/ Wideworld, David Gooley, National Corvette Museum, Indianapolis Motor Speedway, and Superstock

Library of Congress Cataloging-in-Publication Data

McKenna, A. T.
    Corvette / A. T. McKenna.
        p. cm. -- (Ultimate cars)
    Includes index.
    Summary: Surveys the history of the Corvette and its designs, engines, and performance.
     ISBN 1-57765-127-8
    1. Corvette automobile -- Juvenile literature. [1. Corvette automobile.] I. Title. II. Series.
    TL215.C6M35 2000
    629.222'2--dc21

                                      98-4549
                                        CIP
                                        AC

Contents

America's Sports Car

The Corvette is often called America's sports car. A sports car is a fast car that has a sporty look. It is designed for the fun of driving. Sports cars usually have only two seats. Many times the word *sport* is used in the name of the car. For example, *SS* stands for "Sport Sedan" and *GS* stands for "Grand Sport."

General Motors (GM) introduced the first Corvette in 1953. Before the introduction of the Corvette, sports cars were rare in the United States. Some of the sports cars found outside of the United States included Jaguars, Ferraris, MGs, Austin-Healeys, and Triumphs. But these foreign cars were far too expensive for the average American. In the early 1950s, Chevrolet decided it was time to design an affordable American sports car.

On June 23, 1953, the first Corvette rolled off the assembly line in Flint, Michigan. It took the assembly-line crew three 16-hour days to produce this first car. Since then, thousands of Corvettes have rolled off the assembly line in all shapes, colors, and sizes.

Corvettes that are similar to one another are grouped into what is called a generation. A generation can last several years. All the cars in the same generation usually have a similar body shape and style.

Three GM plants have produced the Corvette. The 1953 Corvette was produced at the Flint, Michigan, plant. Then, from 1954 to 1981, Corvettes were produced at the St. Louis, Missouri, plant. Since 1981, Corvettes have been produced at the plant in Bowling Green, Kentucky.

The first Corvette ever made rolls off the assembly line in 1953.

Creating a Car

In order to build a car, it takes hundreds of people, from designers and engineers to mechanics and assembly-line crews. The design department comes up with an idea of how the car should look. The designers usually draw several versions of the car before it is accepted.

Then, they use wood and foam to make a frame that is the actual size of the car. Warm clay is laid on the frame to make a life-size model of the car.

Today, computers can be used to design cars. Once the basic shape of the car is determined, automobile designers use Computer Aided Design (CAD) techniques. The clay model of the car is scanned into the computer. Then, the designer can change the design with the touch of a button.

The car's final design must be approved by the company's executives. Once it is approved,

This woman uses Computer Aided Design (CAD) to design a piece of equipment.

engineers and mechanics work together to build a prototype.

A prototype is a very early version of a car. All the parts on the prototype are tested for strength and quality. The prototype is tested on the race track and on the street to see how it handles. It is displayed at car shows to get people's responses before the actual cars are produced.

After much research is done on the prototype, executives at the company decide whether or not to build the car. If the car is going to be built, changes are made based on the results of the testing and the responses of the people who saw it. Usually, the actual car does not look much like the prototype.

This six-passenger Ford Synergy 2010 prototype car is shown in 1995. The car is designed to use two power sources to get an economical 80 miles (129 km) per gallon.

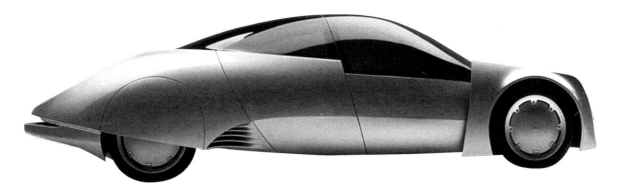

Famous People in Corvette History

There are many people at Chevrolet who helped build the Corvette. The father of the Corvette was chief engineer Zora Arkus-Duntov. He joined Chevrolet in 1953. He worked on every Corvette from 1954 until he retired in 1975.

The head of the Corvette styling, or design, department was Harley Earl. Earl started working at GM in 1927. He saw the need for a sports car in America and had his design staff build the first Corvette for the 1953 Motorama. The Motorama was a car show put on by GM each year to introduce its new cars to the public. The public loved the Corvette.

Bill Mitchell took over as chief stylist after Earl retired. Mitchell joined GM in the 1930s. He had worked under Earl for many years. Mitchell redesigned the Corvette. He named the new design the Sting Ray.

Dave McLellan replaced Arkus-Duntov as chief engineer in 1975. McLellan and his staff used CAD techniques to design the cars. Corvettes from this time on were very high-tech.

Jerry Palmer took over as chief designer after Mitchell retired. Palmer and his designers set out to completely redesign the Corvette. The new model appeared in 1984.

The 1953 Motorama was held at the Waldorf Astoria Hotel in New York City

First Generation

The 1953 models are the rarest of all Corvettes. There were only 300 built. About 200 are known to still exist.

At first, it took three 16-hour work days to finish a car on the assembly line. An assembly line is a system used to mass produce many kinds of products, such as cars. Each worker on an assembly line has a specific job to do.

The workers line up in rows and perform their jobs as the car moves down the line. One worker may put in the steering wheel, while another installs the engine. After a month of producing Corvettes, the assembly-line workers were able to finish three cars in one day.

All the 1953 Corvettes were polo white with red wheels and red interiors. They had black canvas convertible tops. Each car cost $3,513. GM offered only two extra options on the Corvette. A heater cost $91.40 and an AM radio cost $145.15.

The cars had hand-molded fiberglass bodies. They seated only two people—the driver and a passenger. The Corvette had curtains instead of windows, and it had no outside door handles.

The 1953 Corvettes could reach 105 mph (169 km/h) with an engine that was called the Blue Flame Six. These first cars were sold mostly to Hollywood stars and sports figures. Chevrolet wanted the first Corvettes to be seen and admired.

The 1954 Corvette was the first model produced at the St. Louis, Missouri, plant.

Every Corvette made between 1953 and 1962 was a convertible. The 1955 model had the industry's first bucket seats. In 1956, roll-up windows, outside door handles, and seat belts were added. Three different and more powerful V-8 engines were offered. More chrome was added to the Corvette's fiberglass body, giving it a fancier look. An optional removable hardtop was available after 1956.

In 1958, an extra set of headlights was added to the Corvette. They were called quad headlights. The cars were offered in six colors.

The 1962 model marked the end of the First Generation Corvettes. It was the last year that the headlights were exposed.

A 1959 Corvette with quad headlights

Second Generation

The Corvette Sting Ray debuted in 1963. This was the era of rock 'n' roll and drive-in movies. Car manufacturers tried to outdo each other with flashy, glamorous cars that had lots of chrome. The Sting Ray was a real beauty and is still the best-known Corvette of all time. It had a new body design that was lower, thinner, and shorter. The Sting Ray was also more comfortable than previous Corvettes.

In 1963, the Sting Ray was the first Corvette coupe ever offered. Air conditioning and leather interior were also available. The Sting Ray had hidden headlights that disappeared into the hood when they were turned off. The Sting Ray also had a split rear window, called a "stinger."

Today, the 1963 model is one of the most sought after and expensive of all Corvettes. A record of 21,513 Corvette Sting Rays were built in 1963.

The 1964 Sting Ray looked almost the same as the 1963 model. But the rear-window stinger was eliminated in 1964. But the car still kept its name, Sting Ray, until 1967.

In 1965, Chevrolet put a new engine in the Sting Ray. It was called the L78 big block. This engine was large and powerful.

In 1967, Chevrolet wanted to change the Corvette's body style. But, delays left the car looking basically with same with only minor changes. In order to make the car look different, most of the emblems and chrome were removed.

A 1963 Sting Ray

With most of the chrome removed, the Sting Ray was
the cleanest-looking Corvette yet.

Corvette Timeline

First Generation

Second Generation

Third Generation

Fourth Generation

Fifth Generation

Third Generation

A new Corvette was introduced in 1968. It was called the Mako Shark. The Mako Shark was built until 1982. During its production run, Chevrolet built 517,454 Mako Sharks. These cars were very popular, selling a record of 23,562 in 1968.

In 1969, the Sting Ray name changed to Stingray, all one word. The name remained the same until 1982, the year the last Stingray was built.

The Mako Shark

In 1970, a 454 cubic inch (7,440 cubic cm) engine was offered as an option. This was the biggest engine in Corvette history. After the 454 was introduced, the ZL-1 Corvette was produced. This car had an aluminum engine and more than 500 horsepower. Only two ZL-1s were ever built.

In 1971, the Corvette was equipped with the LT-1 engine. This was the last of the fast big block engines.

People were concerned about safety, so the sales of the convertible Corvette dropped considerably. In 1975, the convertible was discontinued.

In 1977, leather seats became standard equipment, and the 500,000th Corvette was produced in May of that year.

In 1978, Corvette celebrated its twenty-fifth anniversary. The Corvette was the pace car for the Indianapolis 500, and the *Wall Street Journal* recommended the Corvette as an excellent investment.

In 1981, the last Corvette rolled off the assembly line in St. Louis, and production moved to Bowling Green.

Fourth Generation

Chevrolet knew that the Corvette needed to be redesigned. So in 1983, the company did not produce a new model. Instead, it worked on the 1984 model.

The 1984 model was lighter and had more interior room than the older models. It was also very fast. The 1984 Corvette could go 137 mph (220 km/h). Chevrolet produced more than 51,000 of the 1984 models. Automotive journalists called this model "King of the Hill."

The Corvette ZR1

In 1986, the Corvette was the pace car for the Indianapolis 500. The year 1986 also marked the first time since 1975 that Chevrolet offered a convertible Corvette. In 1988, Corvette celebrated its thirty-fifth anniversary.

In 1990, Chevrolet offered the new ZR1 Corvette as an option. The ZR1 was a high performance version of the standard Corvette. It had a V-8 engine and could go 179 mph (288 km/h). But, the engine was expensive. It cost $27,016! On July 2, 1992, the millionth Corvette rolled off the assembly line in Bowling Green.

The year 1993 marked Corvette's fortieth anniversary. A special anniversary edition was offered in ruby red. All the cars were ruby red inside and out.

In 1995, the Corvette was again the pace car for the Indianapolis 500. But by the end of that year, it was announced that an all-new Corvette would be coming out in 1997.

Fifth Generation

It was time for a new Corvette, so Chevrolet got its designers to create a new look. Coming up with a design for a new car can take a long time. The work on the new Corvette started in 1989, but the new car wasn't released until 1997. The 1997 Corvette is the first of the Fifth Generation.

The frame of the new Corvette was made using a new process called hydroforming. The main pieces of the frame were made from steel tubes. The tubes were filled with water under high pressure, which made the tubes get larger. Then, the tubes could be bent into the shape of the car.

When redesigning the Corvette, engineers found a way to eliminate 1,400 parts and lower the car's weight by 69 pounds (31 kg). The car's body was made of plastic, not fiberglass. This plastic body made it lighter and stronger. A new engine called the LS1 was installed in the car. The new Corvette posted a top speed of 172 mph (277 km/h)!

Car fans admire the new 1997 Corvette at an auto show.

Corvette Racing

Racing regular street cars, such as Corvettes, became popular in the 1950s. Drivers modified their regular, everyday cars and competed against one another. They installed more powerful engines, wider wheels, and larger tires. Drivers raced in informal races on county roads and at the fairgrounds.

Car manufacturers also got involved in automobile racing at some of the more famous tracks such as Florida's Daytona International Speedway and Sebring International Raceway. In 1956, three Corvettes raced in the Daytona Speed Week. Drivers Zora Arkus-Duntov, John Fitch, and aerobatic pilot Betty Skelton raced the cars. Arkus-Duntov hit a mile record of 150.583 mph (242.288 km/h). Fitch finished third behind two Ford Thunderbirds.

In 1956, Arkus-Duntov designed a Corvette specifically for racing. It was called the SS, and it first appeared on a race track at Sebring. The SS was made of lightweight magnesium instead of fiberglass to keep its weight down.

The car had a headrest, called a pod, that was used as a roll bar for the driver. A roll bar is a piece of the car, usually

U-shaped, that rests above the driver's head. It is padded with foam inside to protect the driver if the car rolls over.

Corvettes quickly made a name for themselves in Sports Car Club of America (SCCA) stock car racing events. Dr. Dick Thompson claimed his first SCCA production-class championship in 1956 while driving a Corvette.

In 1957, the Automobile Manufacturers Association (AMA) banned factory-built race cars. Chevrolet could no

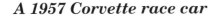

A 1957 Corvette race car

longer build racing Corvettes. But, they still sponsored drivers who raced their own Corvettes.

In 1962, there was a secret attempt to build a world-class racing Corvette, the GS. But because of the AMA's racing ban, only five were built before GM stopped production in early 1963.

Today, Chevrolet is still involved in automobile racing. The Corvette was picked as the pace car for the 1998 Indianapolis 500. A pace car is a regular car that drives in front of the Indy race cars at the start of the race. Once the pace cars does a few laps and then drives off the track, the race begins. The 1998 Corvette pace car cost $47,790. There were 1,163 replicas, or copies, made. Five of the cars were pilot cars that were not sold. But, Chevrolet made 1,158 cars available for sale.

Opposite page: The 1998 Indy 500 Pace Car

National Corvette Museum

If you want to see some of the most famous Corvettes all in one place, visit the National Corvette Museum. The museum opened in 1994 in Bowling Green, Kentucky. Bowling Green has a special significance in the history of the Corvette. It has been the location of the Corvette factory from June 1981 to the present. Many different Corvettes can be seen at the museum, from the early 1953 white convertible to the most current model.

The Corvette Museum and factory are both located in Bowling Green, Kentucky.

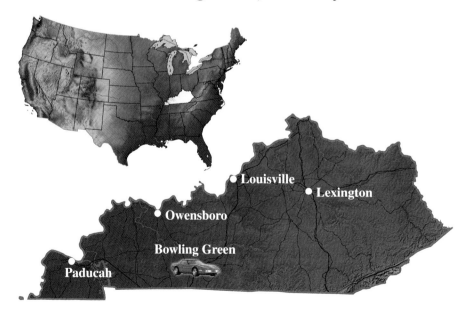

A line-up of Corvettes outside the National Corvette Museum.

Glossary

aerobatics - spectacular feats of maneuverability in an airplane, such as flying upside down and doing loops.

bucket seat - an individual car seat with a back rest that looks like a cutout bucket. Bucket seats come in pairs in the front of a car.

Computer Aided Design (CAD) - computer software that allows a person to design a car by using a computer.

convertible - a car with a top that can be removed. Convertibles can have soft tops or hard tops.

coupe - a car with a permanent top.

debut - the first public appearance.

option - a piece of equipment or a feature on a car that is not included in the basic price. If a buyer wants to add a piece of optional equipment, he or she must pay the extra cost.

performance - the way in which a car handles.

scan - to pass an electron beam over an image. The beam converts the image to electronic properties, which allows the scanned image to be altered or transferred by a computer.

V8 - a V-type engine has two rows of cylinders set at a 60-90 degree angle to one another, and a single crankshaft running through the point of the V. The number after the V indicates how many cylinders the engine has. V8s are V-type engines with eight cylinders. V-type engines may also have four (V4), six (V6), or twelve (V12) cylinders.

Internet Sites

Chevrolet Corvette Homepage
http://www.chevrolet.com/corvette/index-flash.htm

This is the official page of the Chevrolet Corvette from the Chevrolet Web site. Click on the Corvette image to see specs on the latest Corvette model. This site also has a history of Chevrolet cars and links to other GM sites.

The Sports Car Club of America
http://www.scca.org

This is the official site of the Sports Car Club of America. Learn about the SCCA, scheduled racing events, and accredited racing schools. Get information on SCCA pro racing, and a road rally that everyone can compete in.

The National Corvette Museum
http://www.corvettemuseum.com

Visit the National Corvette Museum online. Take a virtual tour of the museum, take a Corvette trivia quiz, and get detailed information on the latest Corvette. This excellent site also has a picture gallery with hundreds of Corvettes to look at, free screensavers and wallpaper for your PC, and a new Corvette puzzle to solve each week.

These sites are subject to change. Go to your favorite search engine and type in "Corvette" for more sites.

Index